Meet the
CHICAGO
BEARS

By
Zack Burgess

NORWOODHOUSE🏠PRESS

CHICAGO, ILLINOIS

NORWOOD HOUSE 🐾 PRESS

P.O. Box 316598 • Chicago, Illinois 60631
For more information about Norwood House Press please visit our website at
www.norwoodhousepress.com or call 866-565-2900.

Photo Credits:
 All photos courtesy of Associated Press, except for the following: Philadelphia Chewing Gum Corp. (6),
 Black Book Archives (7, 15, 18, 22), Fleer Corp. (10 top, 11 bottom), Wonderful World/NFLPA (10 bottom),
 Topps, Inc.(11 top), Crane's Potato Chips (11 middle), Donruss/Leaf–Panini USA (23).

 Cover Photo: Paul Sancya/Associated Press

 The football memorabilia photographed for this book is part of the authors' collection. The collectibles used
 for artistic background purposes in this series were manufactured by many different card companies—
 including Bowman, Donruss, Fleer, Leaf, O-Pee-Chee, Pacific, Panini America, Philadelphia Chewing Gum,
 Pinnacle, Pro Line, Pro Set, Score, Topps, and Upper Deck—as well as several food brands, including
 Crane's, Hostess, Kellogg's, McDonald's and Post.

Designer: Ron Jaffe
Series Editors: Mike Kennedy and Mark Stewart
Project Management: Black Book Partners, LLC.
Editorial Production: Lisa Walsh

LIBRARY OF CONGRESS CATALOGING-IN-PUBLICATION DATA
     Names: Burgess, Zack.
     Title: Meet the Chicago Bears / by Zack Burgess.
     Description: Chicago, Illinois : Norwood House Press, [2016] | Series: Big
        picture sports | Includes bibliographical references and index. |
        Audience: Grade: K to Grade 3.
     Identifiers: LCCN 2015022482| ISBN 9781599537238 (Library Edition : alk.
        paper) | ISBN 9781603578264 (eBook)
     Subjects: LCSH: Chicago Bears (Football team)--Miscellanea--Juvenile
        literature.
     Classification: LCC GV956.C5 B87 2016 | DDC 796.332/640977311--dc23
     LC record available at http://lccn.loc.gov/2015022482

288N—072016
Manufactured in the United States of America in North Mankato, Minnesota

CONTENTS

Call Me a Bear 5

Time Machine 6

Best Seat in the House 9

Shoe Box 10

The Big Picture 12

True or False? 14

Go Bears, Go! 17

On the Map 18

Home and Away 20

We Won! 22

Record Book 23

Football Words 24

Index 24

About the Author 24

Words in **bold type** are defined on page 24.

The Bears
always play
with great
passion.

CALL ME A BEAR

The Chicago Bears love to live up to their name. Sometimes they overpower teams. Other times they outsmart them. They always play with speed and strength. They always play hard. Fans in Chicago love "da Bears" for this. To them, the team is a way of life.

George Halas was the owner of the Bears for more than 60 years. He also coached them from 1920 to 1967. Chicago often had one of the league's top teams under "Papa Bear." The Bears won the Super Bowl after the 1985 season. Two of their greatest players were **Mike Ditka** and Brian Urlacher.

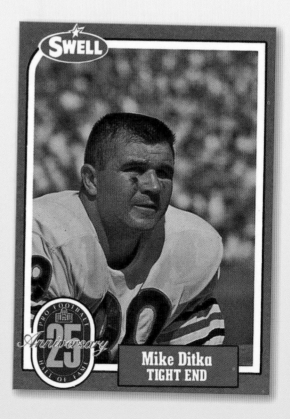

SWELL

Mike Ditka
TIGHT END

Brian Urlacher is ready to make a tackle.

Bears fans love a snowy home game.

Best Seat in the House

The Bears play their home games at Soldier Field. It opened in 1924, and is the oldest stadium in the National Football League (NFL). In the winter, it can also be one of the coldest. The Bears are used to playing in bad weather. This gives the team an important edge.

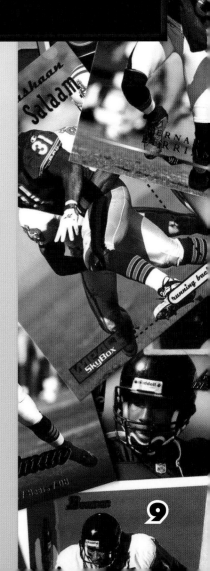

Shoe Box

The trading cards on these pages show some of the best Bears ever.

SID LUCKMAN

QUARTERBACK · 1939–1950

The Bears won four championships with Sid at quarterback. He was one of the NFL's first great passers.

DICK BUTKUS

LINEBACKER · 1965–1973

Dick was the toughest defensive player of the 1960s. He was voted into the **Hall of Fame** in 1979.

GALE SAYERS

RUNNING BACK · 1965-1971

Gale ran with amazing speed and grace. He had a chance to score every time he touched the ball.

WALTER PAYTON

RUNNING BACK · 1975-1987

Walter was the perfect mix of speed and toughness. Teammates and fans liked to call him "Sweetness."

MIKE SINGLETARY

LINEBACKER · 1981-1992

Mike was the captain of the Chicago defense during the 1980s. He made the **Pro Bowl** 10 times with the Bears.

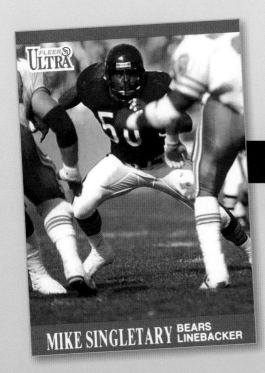

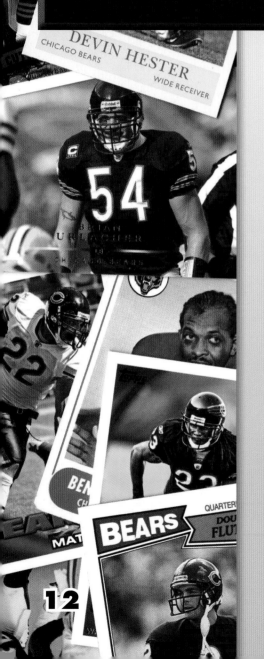

THE BIG PICTURE

Look at the two photos on page 13. Both appear to be the same. But they are not. There are three differences. Can you spot them?

Answers on page 23.

13

TRUE OR FALSE?

Brian Urlacher was a star linebacker. Two of these facts about him are **TRUE**. One is **FALSE**. Do you know which is which?

1 Brian had the most tackles in team history.

2 Brian once swam the entire length of the Chicago River.

3 Brian was an **All-Pro** four times from 2001 to 2006.

Answer on page 23.

Brian Urlacher loved playing for the Bears.

Bears fans fire up the grills on game day.

Go Bears, Go!

You can always tell when the Bears are playing a home game. The smell of grilled food fills the air. Fans have been tailgating around Soldier Field for a long time. Inside the stadium, it's all about football. As soon as the game starts, Bears fans are focused on winning.

ON THE MAP

Here is a look at where five Bears were born, along with a fun fact about each.

 1 JOHNNY MORRIS · LONG BEACH, CALIFORNIA ●————————→
Johnny set a team record with more than 5,000 receiving yards.

 2 RICHARD DENT · ATLANTA, GEORGIA
Richard led the Bears with 17 **quarterback sacks** in 1985.

 3 JIM MCMAHON · JERSEY CITY, NEW JERSEY
Jim guided the Bears to their first Super Bowl victory.

 4 DEVIN HESTER · RIVIERA BEACH, FLORIDA
Devin returned 13 punts for touchdowns for the Bears.

 5 BRONKO NAGURSKI · RAINY RIVER, ONTARIO
After his football days, Bronko became a world champion wrestler.

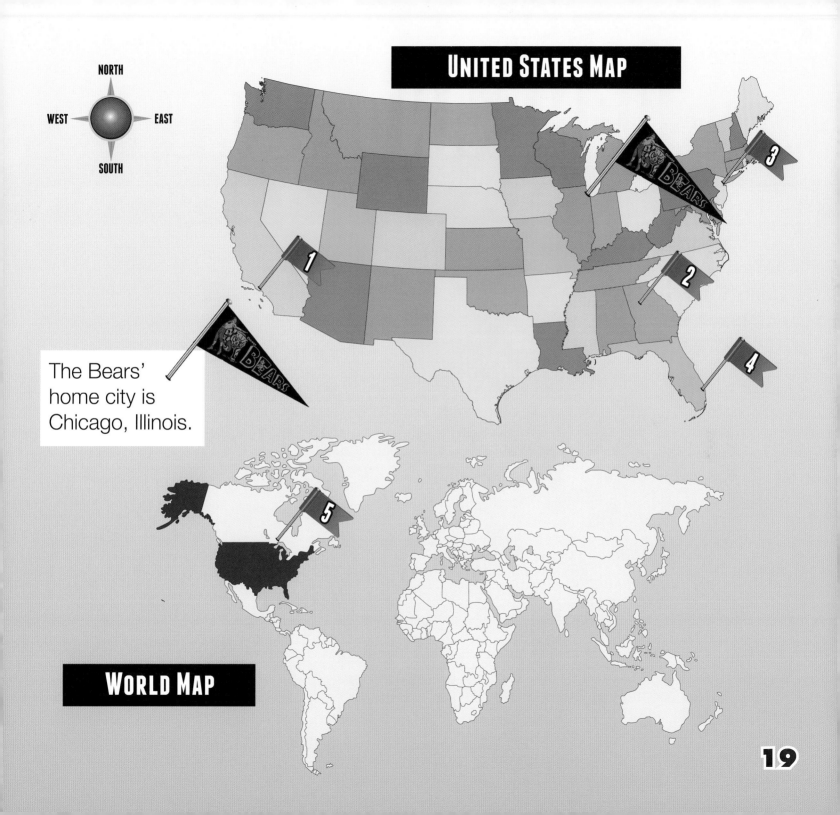

NORTH

WEST ← → EAST

SOUTH

The Bears' home city is Chicago, Illinois.

WORLD MAP

HOME AND AWAY

Alshon Jeffery wears the Bears' home uniform.

Football teams wear different uniforms for home and away games. The main colors of the Bears are dark blue, white, and orange.

Kyle Fuller wears the Bears' away uniform.

The Bears have dark blue helmets. There is an orange and white **C** on each side. The team has used this style of helmet since 1974.

The Bears have played in the Super Bowl twice. They won the big game in 1986. Before the Super Bowl started, the Bears won eight NFL championships. Those titles came under **George Halas** in 1921, 1932, 1933, 1940, 1941, 1943, 1946, and 1963.

These Bears set team records.

TOUCHDOWN PASSES	RECORD
Season: Erik Kramer (1995)	29
Career: Jay Cutler	150

TOUCHDOWN CATCHES	RECORD
Season: Dick Gordon (1970)	13
Ken Kavanaugh (1947)	13
Career: Ken Kavanaugh	50

RUSHING YARDS	RECORD
Season: Walter Payton (1977)	1,852
Career: Walter Payton	16,726

KEN KAVANAUGH

ANSWERS FOR THE BIG PICTURE
#22 changed to 2, #75 changed to orange, and the goal posts disappeared.

ANSWER FOR TRUE AND FALSE
#2 is false. Brian never swam the Chicago River.

FOOTBALL WORDS

INDEX

All-Pro
An honor given to the best NFL player at each position.

Hall of Fame
The museum in Canton, Ohio, where football's greatest players are honored.

Pro Bowl
The NFL's annual all-star game.

Quarterback Sacks
Tackles of the quarterback that lose yardage.

Butkus, Dick..10, **10**
Cutler, Jay..23
Dent, Richard...18
Ditka, Mike..6, **6**
Fuller, Kyle...**21**
Gordon, Dick..23
Halas, George...6, 22, **22**
Hester, Devin...18
Jeffery, Alshon..**20**
Kavanaugh, Ken..23, **23**
Kramer, Erik...23
Luckman, Sid..10, **10**
McMahon, Jim...18
Morris, Johnny...18, **18**
Nagurski, Bronko..18
Payton, Walter..11, **11**, 23
Sayers, Gale...11, **11**
Singletary, Mike...11, **11**
Urlacher, Brian......................................6, **7**, 14, **15**

Photos are on **BOLD** numbered pages.

ABOUT THE AUTHOR

Zack Burgess has been writing about sports for more than 20 years. He has lived all over the country and interviewed lots of All-Pro football players, including Brett Favre, Eddie George, Jerome Bettis, Shannon Sharpe, and Rich Gannon. Zack was the first African American beat writer to cover Major League Baseball when he worked for the *Kansas City Star*.

ABOUT THE BEARS

Learn more at these websites:

www.chicagobears.com • www.profootballhof.com

www.teamspiritextras.com/Overtime/html/bears.html